MW00532543

Typesetting by Janice Lee
Cover Design by Judeth Oden Choi
Cover Art by Kenyatta A.C. Hinkle
Copyediting by Morgaine Baumann
ISBN 978-1-951628-01-7

THE ACCOMPLICES:
A Writ Large Press Book
🐱 🐱 🐱

theaccomplices.org

THE ACCOMPLICES

be/trouble

Make every step cause a little tremor!

bbb

by bridgette bianca

table of contents

section iii: our fallen

section iv: ain't we a dream too

section i: and the living be

at least i can say

i have never wanted to kill myself
but i have
always been keenly aware
that i
could die any day
i have
always been sure something
was trying
to kill me
the
scenarios vary
in almost
all of them
i am afraid
in some of
them
i am
fighting
in all of
them
i lose
but i never
give up
so maybe i
win
after all

this is a
strange conversation

to have
with strangers
but i've
always thought eulogies
were for
the people who never knew you well

they say
malcolm
knew his journey was ending
martin knew
he wasn't long for this world
no i don't
think myself a martyr
i am merely
a black woman
which means
the same thing
where i
come from
that
translation is not my fault
it just is

and if it's
not death
then what
is it

lesson number one

says
step outside of your experience
and again
someone
shakes head
but me
shakes
but me
shakes
but me
shakes
but me

says again
firmly
this time
gently
this time
emphasizes each word
mimes with hands
step outside of your experience

lifts leg
a sad excuse for a fly girl
kick steps into another spot
for the visually inclined
watch my body
watch my mouth
form this concept
step out of your experience

this is you
takes out frying pan
this is your brain on selfish
bashes you over the head
this is you
opens jet magazine july 24 1964
this is your heart on compassion
flips to picture on page eight
this is you
pulls up a social media app
this is your world splintering
plays audio of a 4 year old
mommyidontwantyoutogetshootedmommydontcuss

a saturday night

what do you do when you see lights in the rearview mirror
what do you do when the siren loops around your throat
what do you do when you are on the street in a group of 4
    or more
what do you do when you are alone
what do you do when you know you don't have anything in
    your pockets that can hurt the officer

keep your eyes on the road and find a safe spot to pull over
turn that noise on your radio down before the officer
    approaches your window
didn't they teach you in high school that 4 or more of you is
    a gang
don't you know you shouldn't be out here alone
don't you know that your skin is weaponized in the womb

speak only when spoken to
don't matter that you wasn't doin nothin
don't matter that they be doin this all the time
don't matter that we don't be botherin nobody
don't drop the g's from your ings
don't ask any questions
ask permission to reach into your purse for your wallet
you should just clinch your license between your teeth
and smile while you are doing it
not too hard
black joy is suspicious

keep your hands above your waist
keep your hands on the hood of the car

keep your fingers locked behind your head
take your foot off the gas pedal
keep your feet more than shoulder's width apart
keep your eyes on the ground
do not stare defiantly into the officer's eyes
do not call out in pain when his knee is on your neck
go limp like a rag doll when they grab you
do not bristle when the officer cups your vagina

if you ever find yourself being black on a saturday night
don't

hashtag black girls are real

there's a lot of talk
about magical black girls
who float on clouds of vaporized melanin
whose skin is a never ending sepia rainbow
where are the girls
who feel invincible when their eyebrows are fleeky
and their edges are laid
girls in nameplate gold necklaces and earrings
copper wire wound around their braids
with burnt tips
where are the girls who pop their gum
and smack their tongues
and kiss their teeth
to punctuate
to add emphasis
where are the girls
who never get to be girls at all
they are females
with the tone of bitch
they are das my bitch
with the tone of homie
they are she the homie though
with the tone of lover
do we still love her

girls with praying hands behind their ears
and rosaries on their ankles
girls with script on the small of their backs
or did we decide they weren't magic too

do they have to have flowers in their hair
fake freckles splashed across their nose and cheeks
can they have a constellation
of hyper-pigmentation
on their foreheads
what about the girls
in straight backs and fades
the girls in fresh j's
and timbs
girls who sound less like tinkling glass
and more like the kind of bass
in trunks
that makes earrings shake
bamboo of course
at least two pair
do they have to listen to alternative music
and dance like they have fairy wings
can they buck and twerk
get hype when they hear the opening strings
of a cash money record
or the horns calling for spottieottiedopaliscious angels
lips pursed in concentration
tongues out
daring you to get like them

girls with mile long lashes
that sweep you off your high horse
girls rocking the kind of colorful cornrows and braids
that you will call ratchet until they storm the runways
that you will call ghetto until they are dubbed unicorns
when on somebody else's head
girls who flash their grills when they stuntin
and pose so you know their nails is done

and snatch the air when they speak
are those girls just as magical

are they too loud for you
when they greet each other
are they doing too much for you
when they get
a little recognition
when they ask for
a little more money
when they demand
a little more respect
do they get to shine too
or are they too bright for you

i would say make room for them
but it don't matter because these black girls are bustin through
so make way for them
roll out a carpet of crown royal bags
make sure there are lemon pepper wings on the menu
and hennessey in their cups
and watch them work
their magic

the way she's always paying for a debt she never owed

i have been thinking a lot about black girls
black girls who just want to go home
who don't want to go home
who can't
black girls with no homes to go back to
black girls who make a home wherever they rest their heads
black girls who don't rest

i have been thinking a lot about
black girls in floral crown filters on missing flyers
using geotag filters without alerting their captors
tucking and rolling out of their own trunks
raising their daughters while locked away in basements
black girls in polaroids in the grim sleeper's garage

i have been thinking a lot about
black girls in freakum dresses and fuck me pumps
working western avenue and century boulevard
black girls who use what they got to get what they want
who have to hold their piss while they dance for tips

i have been thinking a lot about
black girls shifting ribs with waist trainers to survive
black girls floating disembodied atop phat asses to survive
wanting so badly to be instagram baddies
wanting so badly for sugar daddies
wanting so badly for daddies
black girls who stiffen when their daddies hug them

i have been thinking a lot about
black girls scarred
everywhere
but their faces
so they can stay pretty
black girls scarred
everywhere
especially their faces
so they can stay ugly
black girls who want good hair
who think their hair is an impediment
who think their skin is an impediment

i have been thinking a lot about
black girls who don't get to be beautiful
who don't get to be carefree
who don't get to be magic
i have been thinking a lot about
black girls who don't get to be girls

to amiri/with love

love is bullshit
unless it is
thick like
granny's biscuits
piled high on a plate
ready for sopping
breakfast syrup
or gravy at supper
fuck love
unless it is useful
not just convenient
and shudders strangely
free from pupae
during
darkness
flutters shyly
into the light
flitting onto
eyelids
and high cheekbones
gifts from the ancestors

we need black love
like fists
pounding hearts
until tender
until melting
love smearing
widow's peaks

with cupid's bows
love warmed and
smoothed
into elbows
resting on tables
and behind knees
bumping beneath

put it on them love
strip them naked to the universe
another badass black love
cracking open
hard shells
of history and heartbreak
of dishonesty and distrust
of fear
black love be-bopping jazz
into discourse
strumming blues into
discord
bumping funky
on the one

let no love poems be
written unless they can
exist freely and
and flop
sloppy
on a couch
before showering off
a long day
let no love poems be written
unless they are free of

pretense
and pretenders
let black people understand
they are the lovers
and the love
the leavers
and all that is left
the writers and
what is right
and all the lovely
in the world

we want a black love
and a black world
let the world be a black love
language
and let all black people speak it
silently
and loud

we are the people darker than blue

during orientation they told me
this job isn't for people with thin skin
so every morning i zip myself into
this melanin rich life and
ready myself for the day ahead
my superiors warned me
the public will say nasty things
they will question my intentions
tell me that i don't belong here
they will antagonize me
they will target me to make a point
they will draw me into altercations
just to turn around and shout injustice
when i defend myself
the public is ungrateful
they do not honor my sacrifice
i've been making america great
for over four hundred years
the thank yous are few and far between
and even then they are hollow

double jeopardy

shirtless black

boys in blue

lining the curb

blocking the street

why did you stop us

what do we have here

just a couple of
thugs

patrolling the streets

looking for trouble

but haven't you

been there before

had enough of this

why are you fighting

stop resisting

die

habitual

be swingin we
be down we
be kickin we
be drowned we
be livin we
be tryin we
be runnin we
be dyin we

*section ii: this much i know
is true*

nikki-maya/mother's day

and he said
you pretty full of yourself ain't chu
so she replied
i am so hip
gold was laid across
the arch of my back
the swing of my waist
the rise of my breasts
does it come as a surprise
the meeting of my thighs
giving divine perfect light
and all that's black within them
created heaven and earth
does my sassiness upset you
it ought to make you proud
even my errors are correct
you wouldn't be nobody
except by my permission
now you understand
i am the one
the dream and the hope
i am so perfect so divine so ethereal so surreal
i am bad
she said
i'm a woman

the grind

my sleep paralysis has always felt like
somebody pinning down my shoulders
sounds like ambulance sirens
and the whir of helicopter blades
my auntie told me to just
say my prayers
and relax
but have you ever seen how tightly
old women clutch their bibles
clutch their rosaries
clutch their children
when they are praying
and afraid

the first funeral i remember
i was maybe 5 or 6
my sleep paralysis feels like my grandmother
in the lobby of a funeral parlour
hugging me to her bosom
until her perfume and humidity made me dizzy
my sleep paralysis feels like waiting at a window
and staring out into the rain
as a train rumbles by
and i don't know if i'm screaming
or if it's just the wind

i discovered in high school
that if i dig my nails into my forearm
i won't go into a deep sleep

i used to think all i needed was a dream catcher
so i fashioned one out of
the shadows my lamp cast
against the walls
imagined my bad dreams
clinging to the web
then sliding down the feathers like
blood
on a dangling hand

this is what keeps me up at night
imagination
roping like okra
in a gumbo
of my memories
brought to a slow boil
over low heat

what doesn't kill you makes you lucky

i thank my mother
for never teaching me
to love a man
when
his voice is rough
from brown liquor
his words
knotting together
and pulling themselves
taut
around my throat
a man who parts lips
with bare knuckles

i thank my mother
for never teaching me
to love a man
when
his footsteps
are war
when his breathing
sounds like ticking
when his eyes
pass over me
like a sniper's scope
searching for his next target
and the softest parts of me
know

the sharpest parts of him
too well

i thank my mother
for never teaching me
to love a man
when
he's so used to
my crumpled body on the ground
that he resents me
when i'm on my own two feet

i thank my mother
for never teaching me
to love a man
who says he will love me to death
because she's seen women
love men
who never broke that vow
until there was nothing left
to love
to live
not even themselves

i thank my mother for saying
girl
if he ever call himself
jumping on you
you better
knock the hell out of him
and keep on knocking
until the devil answers the door

as the wolf picks his teeth with our bones

a man i once respected said
he was tired of everything
being blamed
on the big bad white man
with the haughtiness
of a white woman
in line behind me
at the grocery store
running her basket
into my butt
because she is tired of me
perhaps
i am keeping her from
avocado toast
or she thinks
black ass is so big
and round
and inanimate
that i can't feel the metal
banging into my tail bone

he said this like
two white men
backing into a compact space
parking their pick-up truck
over the line
the driver neglecting to catch his door
before it bangs into

my small hatchback
forcing me
to back out
and park somewhere else
lest i never make it out
into the world

he said this like
i could actually do anything about it

he said this
in a room filled
with big bad white men
their jowls dripping with
a tone that said
i know you people
get upset over things
like this
but if you were just
calm
you would see
we really saved you
from that savagery
we gave you our god
but you refuse
to worship quietly
like we told you

he said this like
big bad white men
don't actually run the world
he said this like
he wasn't one

he said this like
he wasn't one
now more than ever

a man i used to respect said
he could talk about people of color
and their microaggressions
but he didn't want to add fuel to the fire
he said this like
he had already doused my body
in gasoline
and his tiki torch was getting heavy

he said this like
two warning shots
into my abdomen
like i didn't have a license
for my weapon
like a ta-nehisi coates essay
could be easily mistaken
for a gun

he said this like
the few black people around
would ever feel safe enough
to actually have
an honest discussion about
race
or even say the word
white
without wincing
in anticipation of the lash

he said this like
i better be good
or he'll show me
just what
i'm good
for

every nigga is a scar

niggas think black women will take care of them but we off
    that
when black women are harassed, abused, assaulted, or
    murdered by white people
niggas are silent
when black women are harassed, abused, assaulted, or
    murdered by niggas
they are full of excuses

black women ain't got to do shit but stay black and die
and since they are hellbent on killing us
only thing we really gotta do is stay black

(and staying black don't mean
niggas get to ride our backs
to freedom land
we ain't no mule
but let's talk about the niggas who say they love me)

i am suspicious
maybe the better word is unimpressed
saying you love black women
looks good on a t-shirt
saying black women tried to tell ya'll
looks good in a tweet
packing your event full of black women
don't absolve you of your sin
this ain't no baptism
in this bosom

i am not here to comfort you

truth is
i'm tired of these niggas
who say they love me
so i can save them
before i save myself

and i blamed myself
for doing too much
being too much
feeling too much
believing too much
for having the audacity to hope
for setting highly reasonable expectations
like expecting to be seen
and listened to
and spoken of
believed

but i'm not asking for too much
i know that now
the problem is
i been asking for too little
the problem is
i have to ask niggas for anything at all
niggas never know how to anticipate my needs
meanwhile i know them better than they know themselves
i'm reading them like tarot
like palm
like tea leaves
like bloody rorschach tests on white t's
like midnight skies

and i'm reading these niggas like braille
running my fingers over n'jadaka's scars
(because you already know these niggas favorite character
    was killmonger)
niggas treat me like i am the death and the bondage
i count how many bodies have fallen martyr because of their skin
i wonder which lump of scar tissue over a nigga's heart is
    my name

if my body falls
does it even make a sound
does it sound like niggas give a fuck now
did it even fall if there isn't a hashtag
why don't niggas ever fight for me
show up at the rally
and on the timeline
speak up for me and not over me
lift me on their shoulders so i can see
step back so i can be seen
trust me when i tell them what they're missing
trust me when i tell them that they know better

why do niggas need to have daughters to say they love me
is my only value when i am of a nigga's flesh
when i sprang from a nigga's bone
when i am a lump a clay made in his image
why do niggas only love me when they need me
when they can shapemoldknead me

why do niggas say they love me
but believe womanism comes between us
but believe feminism is a cancer

these niggas can't decide if the black family is terminal
or temporary
(but they know it's my fault when they don't stay)
these niggas think we need them to stay
think we be tryna trap them
think we need to hold them down
my womb ain't no anchor
niggas can float on without me

before you say not all men
i'm talking about these here niggas
who say they love me
(for those unfamiliar
nigga
is what you might call a term of endearment
i call it a term of endurance)
if that makes you angry
like old folks say
hit dogs holla

niggas say they love us but we too angry
say black women be landmines
niggas wanna know why they gotta be so
careful when they walk all over us
like we dirt trails between houses
between the south and south central
like we false floors and wagon bottoms
like get free and go back for my family
these niggas think we the mule and the 40 acres
ain't that bout a bitch

why do niggas who say they love me
only love me once i save them

value me because i can weather a storm
do i have to be a light house
do i have to be a rock
do i have to be a shore
when will niggas decide to be safe harbors
for me

an exasperated black woman said fuck it i'll do it

it is fall
i have recently buried a loved one
it is the morning after
the election
you are disheveled and teary
you assume the pain in my eyes is yours
you hug me
a stranger
you say it's so good to talk to
someone who understands
i don't remember speaking
i don't remember your face
stranger
later
i only realize i am crying
by the look on my students' faces

this is not a poem

it is still fall
someone drove past my window
and shouted
fucking niggers
and only i seemed to hear
it is a few days after
the election
you come to me for confession
you are mad at yourself for being so naïve

i tell you the word nigger is a threat to my safety
you are late and have to go
and i am alone again

this is my life

it is spring
i have buried another loved one
i feel faint after yawning
it is months after the election
you are growing angrier
you ask me if i feel the same
i'd been invisible
but now i was useful
so i say
i am a black woman
and i am invisible again

this is not a poem

it is almost summer
you blurt out
ever since the election
you wake up wanting to kill yourself
and you laugh

this is my life

it is fall
194 black people
have been shot and killed by the police
73 more than the last time i read this
what will that number be by winter

this is not a poem

i had a student
whose father
terry
was shot in the head
while laying face down
with his hands
cuffed behind his back
the police pursued him because
he didn't have the proper reflective lights
on his bicycle

this is my life

you may have noticed that
i like to use my hands when i speak
this can be seen as aggressive
and i might frighten you
into killing me

this is not a poem

do you understand
how taboo it is for black women
like me
to go to therapy
because we are supposed to be strong
for everyone

this is my life

i am sorry
that you only realized
the world was fucked up
when your sisters voted
with their white skin
and not their pink pussies

this is not a poem

while you vomit angst
into my lap
forgive me for not
holding back your hair
in solidarity

this is my life

so i'm a little busy

that good black don't crack

this is a big black greasy poem
full of fat back
in collard greens
and salt pork
in red beans
and a tablespoon of bacon grease
mixed into the cornbread batter
smells like
catfish on good friday
and brown sugar glazed ham on easter sunday
listen closely and you'll hear
the sound a hot comb makes
as it passes through hair
before church and on picture days
this poem feels like blue magic hair grease
on your scalp
royal crown pomade smoothed over
with grandma's hands
this poem smells like
johnson and johnson on baby feet
pink hair lotion
and just for me or pcj relaxer
singed and sweet
slick and shiny
like an s-curl on the first day of school
stiff like sleeping propped up
so you won't smash your curls
this poem looks like a tooth brush
caked with brown gel

for your baby hair
fresh like synthetic braids dipped
in boiling hot water and baby oil
soft and a little crooked
like bangs set on pink foam rollers
or strips of brown paper bags
this poem tastes like
thick cut fries
coated in seasonin salt
in a paper bag
from tams or toms or melo burger
or brolly hut or burger palace #1 or 3
this poem smiles at you
while you chewin
and says
it's good ain't it
i know what my baby like

this is a big black loud poem
full of fuck yous
and i don't take no shit from nobodys
and i shall not be
i shall not be moved
and this little light of mine
this poem sounds like
mumbling through the end
of the third verse
of lift ev'ry voice and sing
and a little less singin
and a little more swingin
and foot stompin
and hand clappin
and a little ass shakin too

this poem sounds like
the whisper of
sooooo many plastic bags
stuffed into one plastic bag
like the way big mama
whispers
who cleaned these greens
without her hearing aid
so she really just
loud as hell
this poem sounds like
the clack and swish of
beads and barrettes and ballies
on the ends of plaits
while double dutching with
plastic jump ropes on
black top
you gotta shush
this poem like it's talking back
to the screen at magic johnson's theatre
this poem is
full of warnings before shopping
like
when we go in this store
don't ask for nothin
don't touch nothin
you hear me
full of nigga i wish you woulds
and a reminder that
no
white people
you can't say nigga
why

because your tongue
forms a noose
when you say it
and i'm the one dangling from your lips
there are better ways to die
white people

as a matter of fact
this is a big black righteous poem
full of mlk portraits on church fans
and again beneath pictures of
brown skinned
silky haired
jesus
above malcolm
in a suit and tie
unsmiling
with a finger at his temple
and barack
in a suit and tie
smiling
and looking like a new penny
this poem looks like your father
in a suit and tie
painting over fresh graffiti
on your garage door
before he takes you to school
every morning
because he works too hard
in that suit and tie
for some little gangstas
to think they own his house
this poem sounds like

reimagined fairy tales
where goldilocks
has locks
and repunzel has cornrows
and ananse can whup aesop's ass
in just one round of the dozens
and yo mama sooooo black
she won't buy you white dolls
even if they come with more accessories
she sooooo black
when people gift you white dolls
she keeps them on a high shelf
until you forget about them
and then she takes them to the good will

this is a big black sweaty poem
full of bus rides down south
or better yet car rides
when the air conditioner stops working
half way through texas
it sounds like everybody holding that note
while listening to frankie beverly and maze
you know the one
it sounds like kool and the gang's summer madness
tastes like koolaid
frozen in a foam cup
tastes like my favorite flavor
red
and aunties laughing on the front porch
little cousins screaming through sprinklers
on sunday afternoons
looks like an uncle's special twist on the electric slide
that has him icing his knee before the day is over

this poem feels like
the way the other dominoes on the table
tremble
when somebody yells
gimme fitteen
while slapping bones
feels like being pulled close
in somebody's basement
and slow dragging to songs older than you
like you think you grown
whispering and giggling into the phone
hot against your ear
so your family don't hear
like you think you grown
smells like all day over a barbecue pit
making sure to flip the chicken
so it won't stick to the grill
like your shirt sticks to your back
like thighs in short shorts and skirts
on leather seats
while you cruise the boulevard
like you think you grown

slathered in coconut oil
and shea butter
smothered in vaseline
and cocoa butter
this poem that good black that don't crack

and don't you forget it

on your mark

my father was a track star
and i tried
it
but every
heavy footed step
and every
heaving breath
and every
hair reverting drop of sweat
proved that
it wasn't for me

i still
haven't found a form of running
that didn't
look like i was surely dying
i can't
ignore my brain telling me to stop
whatever it
is i'm doing that is causing me
so much pain

i'm trying to remember when i started apologizing for my body (aka shit people say to fat girls)

when i was a kid
people would say
don't worry
i bet you're going to be tall like your dad and
grow into all of that
stretch all of that out
all of that body
that chubby
that husky
emerge from that baby fat cocoon

but i didn't need to learn
how a punnet square worked
to know that i would never be tall
and no growth spurt would save me from
being the fifth grade fat girl
with low self esteem
and
no growth spurt would
puberty me
into a teenage hottie with a body
or a honey or slimmy or shawty
or whatever pretty girls were called in the 90s
no
i would always be fat
i was sure of it
but i said

yeah
when i grow up
i'm going to be tall
because i knew it made other people feel better
made them feel less guilty for
judging and hurting my fat little feelings
one day i would be a grown up lady
and i would be skinny and beautiful

and i would thank them for reminding me
that i needed to go easy on those cookies
and not stuff myself
even though i picked at my food and ate like a bird
and to only order a kids' meal even though i was over the age
because that should be enough
and if i wanted boys to look at me
i had to think about my body
and oh is that a shape coming in
i knew it
oh your breasts are so big now
are you poking out your chest
what's wrong with you
it's not ladylike to wear oversized t-shirts
don't you want the boys to see you are a woman now
isn't that shirt a little low
wear a bra around the house
don't you want to put on a sweater
that shirt is too thin
i can see the outline of your _____
don't you ever think about trying clothes that fit like this
and accentuate your _____
minimize that belly
nobody wants a girl with a gut hanging all out of her pants

why don't you wear jeans anymore
you know just casual
how you young folks do
why are you always in old lady dresses
hey we haven't spoken in a while
i just want to tell you about this new thing i'm doing
it would be perfect for you
you pay for the shakes every week
and i would be your nutritionist and trainer
i know we never talk about your weight
but i think i know what your problem is
i never see you eating salads
aren't they so refreshing
i never see you eating
i was watching you eating
and it hit me that your diet isn't balanced
yes i was eating the same thing but my metabolism
where do you get your confidence
how can you be so confident
when you are going to die
yes we're all going to die
but who wants to die fat
people might say
did you see the size of that casket
think of the example you are setting for the younger
     generations
baby you are too young to be this fat
i'm telling you now to get that weight off of you
before you're my age and fat like me and miserable and
     lying about your size
i even cut the tags out of my jeans
are you pregnant
if you were how would you know

what is your goal weight
don't i look so fat in these jeans
let me be fat and get something for desert
oh my god i feel so fat and ugly today
i better get in the gym so i can be snatched
don't worry girl
if he don't love you for you then fuck him
i better lose this weight before he sees me naked
and i fuck him
i heard fat girls give the best head
because they always hungry
i heard they the biggest freaks
ugh i bet they smell
can you even see your _____
that's not thick
that's obese
don't no dude want to pick up a chick over 200 lbs
excuse me excuse me
i like em thick ya heard me?
well fuck you fat bitch
that's why you can't get a man now
you gotta keep your looks fresh so your man's eyes don't
    wander
make the effort to make him stay
at least your hair always cute
i have to say you dress so well for a big girl
you have such a pretty face for a big girl
don't worry
it's the inside that counts
i bet if i cut her open cakes and pies would fall out
my profile clearly states that i like working out
you look like you haven't seen a treadmill in years
why are all your profile pics from the breasts up

i'm not embarrassed to be seen with you in public
i just think we'd be more comfortable at home
i always secretly had a crush on you
but i didn't know what my boys would think
but fuck it i'm grown now
and all their baby mamas got fat after having kids anyway
do you want to do a challenge with me on instagram
hashtag gym flow
i wonder if that tea really works
i bet it's mostly water weight
have you ever considered surgery
i heard they make your stomach the size of a peanut
does that mean you only eat peanuts
why are you so afraid to open up
just be cool
you're so unapproachable
yo when i said you was pretty it was just
like a friend
i asked you out as a joke
if you want a chance with me you have to lose 80 pounds
call me when you get your life together
oh fat girls wear halter tops now
look at you girl
large and in charge
you know i'm just playing with you

yeah
i would say
i can't wait until i grow up

section iii: our fallen

to reap

how curious
to find you here
picking through
the bones of our dead
your fingers
tacky with blood
and guile
fumbling for
something supple

and who will be next

we keep planting
these black bodies
over and over again
hoping they'll bring us
fruit
one day
but all i see are
rows of
smoke
all i smell is
tear gas
someone is telling us to
move on
to push our worries
back into the earth
but what are we to do
with these bones
we till this soil
for the new season
forgetting
last year's
attempts
and there
these black bodies
gleaming white
in the sun
these bones
just won't stay
down

the talk

(lesson number one)

no toy guns
no running in public
no hands in pockets
no outside voices

act like
you got
the sense
god gave you
act like
you been
somewhere
act like
you got
somewhere
to be

(act like you got a mama who raised you within an inch of
     your life)

don't cut up
in front of these
white people

(do you want them to take you away from me)

tie all bags at the top
before entering

don't touch anything
you don't plan to buy

(didn't i tell you to take your hands out of your pockets)

don't swing your arms
when you walk
take your hands off
your imagination
you acting like you grown
mind your mouth
i swearfogawd
you bet'not let me catch you
doing something you ain't s'posed to

(and you better not have nothin in your pockets)

i don't care what
they said to you
i don't care what
the others
get away with
they are not my child
i don't care if
their parents don't hold their breath
when they see a face
flash across the evening news
or their newsfeeds

(just bring your tail home)

i don't
want you out of my sight

because if i can't
see you
if i can't
hear you breathing
then every siren
is always headed
in your direction

every face in despair
every body on the ground
every bowed head in cuffs
every gasp for breath
every plea for mercy
every hand up in the air
every fist balled in anger or fear
looks like it belongs to you
and you are mine

(but they can take you away from me don't you know that)

you've got to know better
do better
be better

(and even that won't really save you but what else can i do)

so get your behind back in this house
and don't make me tell you again

now i play black mama crying over dead son

now i lay me down to weep
my body
next to a body of my body
next to my boy
can i return him to me

i mop his blood with my hands
can i absorb him
can i make him over again

if i lie still as he
maybe death will take me
believe me dead
instead

can i cup his face and scream
air back into his lungs
so he can catch my breath
as his breath
am i not the wind

he is my world
surely
i am just a moon
surely
he is the sun
but he is so cold

give us this day/death is our daily bread

joshua williams was murdered in front of my home
three days before father's day
i was
on my way to buy my father a gift
i wonder
if joshua had a daughter
i wonder
if she made him a colorful construction paper tie
like i once made for my father

joshua williams was murdered in front of my father
he was tending the garden
my father
i heard joshua had a gun
maybe it was in his waistband
maybe it was in the pocket of his hoodie
maybe it was just the other boys shooting
i'm not sure
i wasn't there
i just smelled his insides splashed across the outsides
i passed his sneaker in the street

i have to confess
this is a selfish ass poem

i have blushed at so many boys
with guns in their waistbands
i have said

have a good day
to my father
so many mornings

sometimes i fall asleep praying for god
to bless each member of my family
worried
that if i don't say their names
god might snatch them from me
while i sleep

i wonder
if joshua ever said his prayers that way

i read the la times homicide report
for fun
i read the la times homicide report
so i can stop being afraid
i am desensitized as a safety mechanism
i live comfortably between orange and red alert

james baldwin was right
i am in a constant state of rage

joshua williams was murdered in front of where my heart is
i have been holding back a scream
and fear the scream has died
and is now just the air used to read this
i am afraid the air will go away
i am afraid the air will expel
i am afraid the air is a black exhaust
i am black and exhausted

and it took me two months to stop hiding in the bathroom
every time my father walked outside
i think it took a bit longer for my mother
to stop watching him from the window
sometimes i think she still does
looking
when she thinks we're not
i wonder
how long it took joshua's girl
i wonder
how long it took joshua's mother
i wonder
how long it took joshua's future
to stop looking for him

position open until filled

blank
was a good blank
blank
had a troubled blank
blank
was a mother of blank
blank
had a promising blank
blank
planned to blank
blank
was new to blank
blank
knew it was time to blank
blank
wasn't supposed to blank
blank
was protecting blank
blank
was walking in a blank
blank
had a shiny blank

that looked like the barrel of a blank
that looked like a the hilt of a blank

i have mistakenly written black
instead of blank
no less than blank times

wait no less than
blank times

i ask you what difference does it make
this is not a madlib
we are all mad here

for colored girls when rainbows don't lead to nothin and fairy godmothers ain't real

like most fourteen year olds
naika venant had a facebook page
she shared everything with the world
on january twenty-second
naika venant livestreamed her suicide

i didn't know her
but don't i
i don't know what she looked like
when she cried out
in foster care
or while being assaulted
or while insulted by her mother
i don't know what she looked like
while her mother typed
u keep crying wolf
u dead
u will get buried
life goes on
as she watched naika
i don't know what she looked like
hanging there on the screen

but don't i
i know what she looked like in a selfie
smiling up at the camera
angled above her head

light filling her face
like she held the sun in her small hands

naika
wanted to love
needed safety
wanted affection
naika needed somebody to save her
and i did not know her
but don't i
there are a thousand naikas
and each one of them is irreplaceable
naika needed somebody to miss her
and i did not know her
but don't i miss her just the same

freedom

today
i caught myself thinking
kalief would be a beautiful name for a son
what would
my sweet child think
if he sought the meaning of his name
and found images of a handsome boy
tortured and discarded
grown into a man
while in a cage
released
but never truly free

i would tell him
his namesake was a warrior
courageous as they come
and he lost his life
in a battle he didn't pick
on a field already slick with blood
a casualty in a war
he was never meant to win
but he fought anyway
and we fight for him
still

what have they done

i know he was 16
i know he was 18
i know he was 44
and now he is not

he had a name
and now he is
a body
on the asphalt
on 107th and budlong
on west florissant
in front of a convenience store
in the back of a van
at a metro station
at a park

i know bresha was 14
when she saved
her mother's life
by taking her father's
i've never seen a picture of her smiling
i know her heart was broken
i hope they haven't broken her spirit
i have never heard her speak before
i hope they haven't stolen her voice
she is 16 now
and they just gave her back
her body
her life

after they took her
away

i don't know much about him
but his sweetheart's name is bridget too
i followed her on instagram
because her hair was pretty
and when his death appeared
on the news
he looked so familiar
he left this world the same way he came in
naked
and confused
no one can explain where he hid his weapon
but i know they saw it in his skin
they said anthony had bipolar disorder
but he was not mentally ill enough
to take to burger king for a whopper
or to call a sweet boy
or to call an all-american kid
or to tackle to the ground
or to pepper spray or tase

i didn't know much about him
but out of respect for him
i will never stand for their anthem
he was a veteran
he served this country in the air force
and when they were done with him
they took the trigger out of his hand
they placed a trigger in his mind
said he was not mentally fit enough to serve

the officer had pepper spray
and a taser
anthony had ptsd
the officer said he was on pcp
i don't know which bullet killed him
the first or the second
he had pepper spray and a taser
the officer was afraid
the 911 caller said
anthony needed medical attention
the operator said he was suspicious
i hesitate before calling the police
because i don't want to kill anybody

anthony was mentally ill
he didn't know that was white people shit
black people don't get to be mentally ill
we get to be crazy
we get to be deranged
we get to be monsters
we get to be exactly what they thought we were
we don't get to plead our cases
in front of a jury of our peers
they have to put us down
before we get to be too dangerous
if allowed to speak
we may incriminate them

anthony was 27 years old
i don't know much about him
he was a person
and they took his mind
they took his body

they took his life
away

and they know exactly what they have done

disaster

he asks me
did you hear there was another
shooting
and i answer
yeah
with a small sigh
kind of lazy
like he asked me
if i saw the final score
of the laker game
or if i ever felt alone
words like
church shooting
school shooting
massacre
lone wolf
spree killer
unarmed black man
gang related
these phrases roll out of our mouths
like the weather
like did you hear the rain last night
no
i was sleeping
i heard about the storm
when i woke up
i didn't hear the tree crash through the roof
i didn't see the water
creeping under the door

until i heard the splashing
this violence has become
a flash flood in the night
pulling us all down river
letting us out into the ocean
the constitution guarantees us
the right to paddle
but
we need dams
we need levees
we need to drain
this country
like a blister
clear out the infection
dress the wound
we are feverish
where i'm from we'd say
the block is hot
we are burning
i say
i haven't been watching the news
i've had enough death for the day
haven't you

section iv: ain't we a dream too

i want the world to see

seven

i don't get to talk about hitting the ground
or the hands that pin me there
everybody else gets to body bag me
slip me out when they are bored
fidget spin me and see if i'm as pliable as their laws
see if the black woman really is the mother of the world
explore my womb looking for the big bang or god

am i making you uncomfortable

six

did you know planned parenthood offers more than abortions
did you know wic don't pay for diapers
did you know formula is expensive
and i can't breastfeed my baby in private because i have to work
and i can't breastfeed my baby in public
because you only like my titties when they bouncing in your
face

am i making you uncomfortable

five

judging me for putting juicy juice in my toddler's sippy cup
like i got time to worry about high fructose corn syrup or
artificial food coloring

when you just legalized marijuana but my son is still getting
stopped and frisked
how dare you paint white mothers addicted to opioids with
the finest brushes and oils
after you slammed me into the concrete so many times i
couldn't help but have crack babies

am i making you uncomfortable

four

you take my kids and send them hurtling across the universe
lie and call them shooting stars when they're just
plummeting asteroids
and you judge me because my babies make craters they can't
lift themselves out of by their bootstraps
because you cut those too

am i making you uncomfortable

three

due to a surplus of black children they are inexpensive to
adopt
people treat cheap things like they are disposable
like drive a car full of black children over a cliff

am i making you uncomfortable

two

this is what it feels like to be a woman in a land more
concerned with putting restrictions on my pussy than

assault rifles
this is what it feels like to be anything but white in a
country that values confederate monuments more than my
child's flesh

am i making you uncomfortable

one

good

title

this is why mamie left emmett's casket open

there goes the neighborhood

first
they came for our bodies
snatched my nose
right off my face
then placed
a forearm
across my windpipe
clamped a sweaty palm
over my mouth
and said
the use of force
was justified
because i insisted on breathing

maybe it started with the ships

first
they came for our bodies
laid us down like
railroad ties
carved a path west
on our backs
filled their coffers
with gold
and our bellies
with god
and other white men
for us to fear

maybe it started with the ships

first
they came for our bodies
my body looked out of place
in that car
how could i afford it
it must be stolen
i was stolen
so they made me pay for it

my body looked out of place
in that neighborhood
when all along
my body was out of place in this country
they uprooted and planted my body here
because it was fertile
and would yield
more crops
cotton
rice
sugar
tobacco
independence from britain
a more perfect union

maybe it started with the ships

first
they came for our bodies
i cradled this economy
and it nursed at my breast
it continues to reach under my clothing

to be pacified and soothed
never satisfied
this country throws tantrums
because i won't bare it all for their profit
forgetting that prisoners cannot consent
and my refusal never stopped them
from taking my body
before

maybe it started with the ships

first
they came for our bodies
then
they came for this land
maybe it started with music festivals
extravagant dioramas on stolen grounds
where they cosplay in bejeweled bindis
and dreamcatcher earrings and buddha tattoos
and kush and coronas and cocaine
limbs flailing like tattered flags
they dance to
rhythms they beat out of indigenous bodies
in boarding schools
the audacity of stars and stripes draped over their shoulders
and eagle feathers in their hair

maybe it started with the ships

maybe it started with a coffee shop
on a corner that's been empty since the riots
the shadow of a mini-market
where the shopkeeper

called elderly black women
mama
out of respect and limited english
and out of neglect and unlimited anguish
we'd burned it in effigy

maybe it started with the ships

maybe it started with a new boutique
with high prices and sparse racks
no lay away in their store policy
no habla espanol
no patience for poverty
new age vending machines
loot bodegas
fusion food trucks shame
sistas selling cocoa bread
with butter and honey
for the sin of gluten
the man selling oranges and cherries
on the boulevard
cannot compete
with the new organic farmers market

maybe it started with the ships

first
they came for our bodies
then
they came for this land
gave it a hashtag for a name
the new world
south harlem became soha

spanish harlem became spaha
columbia heights dc became cohi
south central los angeles became sola
como se dice bullshit
these hipster hideaways
upper middle class settler colonies
bourgeois urban safaris
the ghetto has become a life hack
the homes we made
in the barrel's bottom
after white flight
are now best kept secrets
and the blocks
where black and brown boys learn to click-click-bang
and get stuck
become plymouth rocks
for millennials wanting more bang
for their buck

maybe it started with the ships

this must be how the ancestors felt
when they saw sails in the distance

the pilgrims have found us again
and this time
they say they don't need our bodies
just the warm streets we leave behind

ego-trippin

if i ruled the world
there is nothing
i would really change
well maybe
i would get rid of
a particularly
orange faux/foe
but then again
if i ruled the world
there would be no need
because characters like him
would only exist
in post-apocalyptic films
and then again
post-apocalyptic films
might not exist
because we wouldn't need
racial allegories
veiled in alien skin
because racism
the father of race
would've curled up and died
in whichever white man's mouth
it was born into
and perhaps
the white man would not exist at all
because he would not have had
africa's resources
to build his wealth
or dominance over the world

because see
i
a black woman
would rule the world
and people would know
the black woman as god
and regard her image
not with fear or even reverence
but with grace
but then again
perhaps
if i ruled the world
no one would know
me
need me
praise me
ask me
for anything
love
help
or mercy
instead
they would
simply know
the god
in themselves
and find a stillness
satisfaction in themselves
and then finally
maybe
black women
could rest
and say
it was good

repeating a lie don't make it true

the constitution is not the bible
the amendments are not the commandments
your forefathers are not
father god
jesus christ
or the holy spirit
they're not even fallen angels
they were men
flesh and blood
do not take them in wafer or wine
they will neither feed your soul
nor nourish your spirit
you will starve waiting for them
to deliver you
from the browning of america
there is no red capped mothership
coming to take you to the promised land
speaking of promised land
as in acres
what you got on my 40 homie
but i digress
this land of
milk is spoiled and spilt
this land of
honey is no more
your industrialization
has killed the bees

your leaders are false prophets
with more concern for lost profits

and launching rockets
and lining their pockets
with the nra's blood money
than the loss of school kids
isn't it funny
that the kings you serve
are jesters

these dreams you have
of a simpler time
where people weren't so sensitive
and offended
and triggered
they are dust
they are filament
they are figments of your imaginations
do you understand they are a mirage
there is no great american paradise
nestled in the past
waiting to come around again

your flag is not the crucifix
when i kneel in its presence
i am not repenting
i am perhaps tying my shoe
or ducking to miss
the bullshit spewing from your mouth
your anthem is not the lord's prayer
it is a fairy tale
it is a lie
and repeating it
don't make it true

and so
we the people
created equal
have suffered
under evils insufferable
and declare
these men
were then and are now still
unfit to be rulers of free people
and so
charge them with
breaking and entering our lands
breaking and entering our minds
breaking and entering our bodies
breaking and entering our bodies
breaking and entering our bodies
and we
the jury of their deepest
the jury of their darkest
the jury of their fears
find them guilty
and you
complicit
in their sin

we will bring them to heel

what you say to me boy
you black sons of bitches
with your pants half off your ass
with your gold chains
with your nappy hair
and your multi-million dollar contracts
on your knees demanding more humanity
haven't i given you enough
i brought you here to work
do what you are told
when i say get down
i mean stay down
don't you get smart with me
when i say jump
you say how high
when i say throw
you say how far
when i say run
you say how fast
and when i say stand
god damn it you stand boy
and you better do it like i told you
or i will snatch you right off the field
and take that football out of your hands
so you can't feed your family
you better do it like i told you
or i will snatch you right out the fields
and take those cotton bolls out of your hands
so you can't feed your family

remember
a lazy nigger is a dead nigger
and a dead nigger don't make me no money
but i will make an example out of you
and those left behind
will work twice as hard
to compensate
for my loss of property
do you hear me boy

you can't spell patriot without r-i-o-t

they won't call it war
but we brace ourselves
for attack
we stay ready
so we ain't gotta get ready
and yet we are unprepared

they are heavily armed
we are heavily harmed
the preachers tell us
we are heavenly armed
and they tell us to
forgive
they call for peace and
quiet
but we cannot quiet
we speak out
riot
we come out
riot
we lash out
riot
we reach out
riot
we shout out
riot

and martin said
a riot is the language of the unheard
then james said
it is not the black child's language
that is despised
it is his existence
and before he was amiri
leroi said
let the world be a black poem
and nikki said
maybe i shouldn't write
at all
but clean my gun
and malcolm said
revolution overturns and destroys
everything that gets in its way
and gil said
the revolution will be no re-run
brothers
the revolution will be
live

reason number 72

i will never become president
because
they see me
a
brown
loaf
of a woman
as somewhere soft
they can rest their heads
and warm their hands
and who wants mammy in the oval
mumbling juju under her breath
or screaming bloody murder
and begging you for mercy
as you pull the baby from her arms

i will never become president
because i did that already
sacrificed and made this nation great
for you
the first time around
while my own children went to market
and no one wants
mammy
in the oval
unless she's carrying a tray
or a tune
and if i can't sing
then who cares

what sound i make
when i am wounded
or angry
and besides
i'm tired of cleaning
your messes

a message from uppity negresses

i know what you're thinking when you see me
she think she all that
she think she too good
she forgot her place
she think she better than somebody

well

the elders told me
i had to be
twice as good
twice as nice
twice as smart
twice as fast
twice as strong
twice as clean
twice as polite
work twice as hard
to get half as much
as you

and here i am
lapping you
in every race
outperforming
outlifting
outlasting
outplaying you
in every match
still

fighting
for what you leave
as table scraps

and
you
intellectual
conservative
liberal
progressive
feminist
suffragette
realist
socialist
an ally
are jealous
of my oppression

you hastily throw on
your sheerest victimhood
to prove
you
too
have been discriminated against
someone once called you racist
and you were aghast

you
too
have experienced sorrow and suffering
and only your brown nanny
and only your black mammy
was there to kiss your booboo

you
too
have been offended
by words just as bad as nigger with the hard er
such as
snowflake
mayonnaise
pale face
and becky

you
too
have grappled with the burdens of history
the weight of ancestral guilt
is too much to bear

you are tired of apologizing for your privilege

it is unfair
that we all
have issues
but only i
brown
black
migrant
immigrant
indigenous
imported goods gone bad
exported goods marked return to sender
feather headdress and fried chicken
come home to roost

only i
expect
hand outs
a leg up
a head start
some type of affirmation
of my humanity
because i am lazy

even as i work
twice as hard
am twice as polite
clean
strong
fast
smart
nice
good

and the elders taught me
to be humble
to keep my head down
and you'd never notice me
so i don't dance in the end zone
i don't beat my chest after i score

i just adorn myself
in the kind of things
you would call
tacky
ratchet
ghetto
until you

manifest my destiny
repackage it to be cool
urban
tribal
ethnic

and then you tell me
you didn't even notice i was black
you say we are all one race
all lives matter
i know better but
you demand i concede and repeat
you try to pacify me
with your colorblind mythology

the way you once used christ
on a cross
to tether me
even after the chains
were off

you say you don't notice
but i think you do
so i want you to know
i am all that
i am too good
i know my place is first
and if you have to ask
then i have to confirm
the rumors are true
i am better than you
and you can stay mad

was it good for you/like blood on dry ground

but the world stopped
when our eyes met
he moved slowly
uncertain of my intentions
and i kept my pace
my heart racing

his shirt read
the south shall rise again
the words framing
a faded confederate flag
across his chest

if the south rose again
it would be brown fingers pushing up through the soil
brown legs jumping down from poplar branches
brown arms lifting themselves out of swamps
brown eyes staring out from tar slick patches
brown bodies reforming from the ashes

if the south rose again
it would be my ancestors
returning to slit your throat
cane river would jump its banks
the levees would not hold
from the rush of your blood
and my children would splash and play in it
with smiles on their brown faces

for the nice white ladies on parade

my body is falling
do not step over my body
do not kneel over my body
do not weep over my body
lay on the ground next to me

be a human with me
be skin broken by rough handling
be flesh exposed and grated across cement
be bloody lips and scraped knuckles

do not congratulate yourselves
for donning pink hats en masse
what set you from
be black boys
who pledge allegiance to red or blue
by the age of 10
be black girls
whose names are phonetic
and attitudes are kinetic
be the black fathers
you don't believe exist
be black mamas
with hands on hips
we are not sassy
for your amusement

be down on the ground
with me
even when i'm too loud

and so passionate
it scares you a little
be down on the ground
with me
when i scare you
a lot
remember
i am scary

i am not your brown comfort cushion
i am not your mammy hug
i am not the black receptacle
for your new complicated feelings
about race
after the election
i am not your
imnotracistsomeofmybestfriendsareblack card
do not pull me from your hand
like a draw 4 in uno
i am not your friend
and i am not asking you
to be my ally
i am telling you

get down on the ground next to me
taste your own blood in your mouth
asphyxiate in a pool of your own words
after someone calls you
so articulate
with an air of surprise
impale yourself
on that self-righteous stick
up your ass

wonder how many poems died
while you were busy mourning a black girl in texas
with a slick mouth just like you
a black boy in florida
who looks like your nephew
and another in cleveland
who looks like emmett till
wonder how many poems died
while you stood at your kitchen window
and watched them wash foamy blood into the gutter
wonder if it will be you the next time
remember that you can die for less

malcolm said
if you're not ready to die for it
take the word freedom out of your vocabulary
i say
if you aren't ready to die for my freedom
take the word ally out of your vocabulary

i call you sis because you my sista

she says
black women could've avoided slavery if we were considered
beautiful. men don't hurt women they want to fuck. ex. white
and asian women.

sis
as if black women ain't valued by the amount of pain we can
     handle
as if black men don't tear up
at the thought of how much shit we put up with
while we were waiting on them
to develop into something
we wouldn't mind spending the rest of our lives
chasing
as if black women ain't dismissed as too aggressive and
     emasculating
while simultaneously hypersexual hos and tricks
have you never listened to nina simone's four women
or at least watched a rap video

sis
you need to read more
and maybe look in the mirror
have you ever even met yourself
black woman
you mistake beauty for value
you mistake attraction for value
you mistake erection for value
a man wanting to fuck you

doesn't mean your life is precious to him
let alone your body
it doesn't mean he
respects your humanity
any more than the reverence
he shows his left hand
compared to his right

so let's discuss avoiding
the messy business of slavery
if only we were considered beautiful
by our oppressors
tell that to our foremothers
sis

so according to you
when ol massa was tippin
out the big house and
down to the quarters
if only he had noticed how sunlight
bends and kisses dark flesh
like an overseer's whip
if only he'd lusted over
the strength and shape
of her thighs and hips
as she toted
his harvest
if only he'd seen the bounty
in her bosom
as she nourished his children
while her own children
even the ones he thrust into her
went without

according to you
if only he'd seen her beauty
he wouldn't have hurt her
he would've set her free

sis
please

i bet you still think your great grandma was
lightskin and had good hair
because you got indian in your family
sis you got colonizer in your family
i'm sorry
to disappoint you

if men didn't hurt women they wanted to fuck
then most of us wouldn't even be here
there is no beauty bargain
we can't pretty ourselves out of oppression
langston hughes said
and they'll see how beautiful i am
and be ashamed
but he never said that a man
would be too embarrassed
to stroke your hair after busting your lip
never too sheepish to say he'll never hurt you again
again
and again
sis

did it ever occur to you
that they hurt us because they knew
we were beautiful

because they knew we were majestic
that they did not need convincing
of our humanity because
they knew it all along
no
the work was convincing us
that we were not beautiful
with our full lips and broad noses
so they stretched us over their own faces
into shoe polish caricatures
distorting our features
and made a spectacle of themselves
made us think the joke was on us
in us
we were the joke

and the gag is
sis

east asian women are fetishized
out of their innocence
south asian women are terrorized
out of their brownness
and white women
sis
they've got their own batch of problems
that no amount of hair bleach and self-tanner can fix
and we'll save human trafficking stats for another day

in the end
what the oppressor thinks of you
is really none of your concern
because they are a fickle bunch

and i wouldn't want my humanity
to swing on a hinge of their pleasures
or perversions

sis
think again

some heroes wear their durags with the capes flapping

this is how black people have survived
part one

the colonizers' greatest mistake was
underestimating our power
all they needed to see was our talented tenth
to know that we were
too dangerous to be left
unregulated
unfiltered
unconquered
and so they did
or so they thought

but we still here
still david and his sling
still harriet and her rifle
still john henry with the hammer
still jesse owens whupping a nazis ass
still ali whupping uncle sam's ass
still michael jackson on the moon
still katherine johnson with the math
still michael jordan with the rock
still doctor king taking a knee
still kaepernick taking a knee
still rosa parks taking a seat
still mahalia raining down heaven
still richard pryor raising hell

still fred hampton with a bull horn
still octavia with the pen
still malcolm x headed to mecca
still chadwick at the mecca
still ta-nehisi at the mecca
still morrison at the mecca
still zora when she's laughing
still zora when she's looking mean and impressive
still barack obama on the capitol steps
still audre lorde reminding us that she is not free while any
    woman is unfree
even when her shackles look like cuban links
still assata in exile
still langston in paris
still baldwin in paris
still josephine in paris

the time for running has come to an end
stokely carmichael said
tell them all the scared niggas are dead

we still t'challa to the bullshit
we still jesus on the third day
as you can see
we are not dead

this is how black people have survived
part two

the colonizers greatest mistake was
underestimating our resilience
we been minding our own business
and mining something stronger than vibranium

reaping and sowing something better than king cotton
we been digging for something blacker and slicker than oil

what's understood don't need to be explained
put some respect on our name
we are wakanda
we ain't never been conquered

we been wakanda
death is better than bondage
but you can't chain us
and no matter how hard you try
you can't kill us all
and you can't beat this black off us
and you can't shoot this black off us
and your walls ain't high enough to keep us out
your jails ain't tight enough to keep us in
february ain't long enough to get us right

we be wakanda
just because we be magic
don't mean we don't be real
this ain't no super power
this is black power

acknowledgments

To my parents, Faye and Lee, thank you for believing
in me. To my Aunt Brenda and Uncle Ishel, thank you
for your unwavering support. And to my dear heart, my
grandmother, Elmae, thank you for teaching me that what I
had to say was important, that I was important. Everything
I do, I do in your honor.

To Sanura Williams and Dr. Alisha Brown, thank you for
enduring decades of my terrible poems and being my ad-
hoc managers. To Chenel King, B. A., and Nikki Williams,
thank you for inspiring me with your ambition. To V. Kali
and Jessica "Yellawoman" Gallion, thank you for welcoming
me into the sisterhood of The World Stage.

To my press mates, Rocio Carlos and Rachel McCleod
Kaminer, thank you for pushing me. To Kima Jones and
Jack-Jones Literary Arts, thank you for your work and your
wisdom. Thank you to Joseph Rios, Sara Borjas, Imani
Tolliver, and Natashia Deon for helping introduce this
book to the world. Thank you to Chiwan Choi for asking
about my book when I had just seven poems to my name.

about the author

bridgette bianca is a poet and professor from South Central Los Angeles. She received her Bachelor of Arts in English from Howard University and her Master of Fine Arts in Writing from Otis College of Art & Design. She has performed poetry all around Southern California. Her work seeks to serve the people and moments most forget or ignore.

OFFICIAL

THE **ACCOMPLICES**

GET OUT OF JAIL
* VOUCHER *

- -

Tear this out.
Skip that social event.
It's okay.
You don't have to go if you don't want to. Pick up
the book you just bought. Open to the first page.
You'll thank us by the third paragraph.

If friends ask why you were a no-show, show them
this voucher.
You'll be fine.

- -

We're thriving.

CPSIA information can be obtained
at www.ICGtesting.com
Printed in the USA
FSHW010138110120
65852FS